AMAZING MYSTERIES

FAIRIES

BY MELISSA GISH

CREATIVE EDUCATION   CREATIVE PAPERBACKS

Published by Creative Education and Creative Paperbacks
P.O. Box 227, Mankato, Minnesota 56002
Creative Education and Creative Paperbacks are imprints of
The Creative Company
www.thecreativecompany.us

Design by The Design Lab
Production by Rachel Klimpel
Art direction by Rita Marshall
Printed in the United States of America

Photographs by Alamy (AF archive, AF archive/Film Company
Disney, AF Fotografie, Charles Walker Collection, Science History
Images, James Thew), Deviant Art (WolfWhoSings), Flickr (David
Lee), Getty Images (Glenn Hill/SSPL), iStockphoto (FairytaleDesign),
Mary Evans Picture Library (Medici), Shutterstock (Atelier Sommer-
land), Unsplash.com (Jeff Finley)

Library of Congress Cataloging-in-Publication Data
Names: Gish, Melissa, author.
Title: Fairies / Melissa Gish.
Series: Amazing mysteries.
Includes bibliographical references and index.
Summary: A basic exploration of the appearance, behaviors, and
origins of fairies, the winged, magical creatures known for their
tricks or helpfulness. Also included is a story from folklore about how
fairies learn to fly.

Identifiers:
ISBN 978-1-64026-488-5 (hardcover)
ISBN 978-1-68277-039-9 (pbk)
ISBN 978-1-64000-615-7 (eBook)
This title has been submitted for CIP processing under LCCN
2021937337.

First Edition HC 9 8 7 6 5 4 3 2 1
First Edition PBK 9 8 7 6 5 4 3 2 1

Table of Contents

Fairies are members of a family called *aos sí* (AYS *shee*), or "people of the mounds." These magical beings are humanlike. Some ride on birds or butterflies. Others have wings and can fly. Fairies can make themselves disappear.

Fairies do not like to be seen so will fly away quickly if spotted!

Nature spirits called dryads were thought to live in forests.

Fairies play tricks on humans. They hide tools and cause objects to fall. Not all fairies are nice. Some make will-o'-the-wisps. These lights rise above swamps and **bogs**. They lead travelers into danger.

bogs areas of wet, muddy ground into which a person can sink

Fairies may secretly swap bad fairy babies with good human babies. Old fairies may trade places with newborns. They want to rest and be cared for. Traded fairies are called changelings.

People who thought something was wrong with their baby blamed it on fairies.

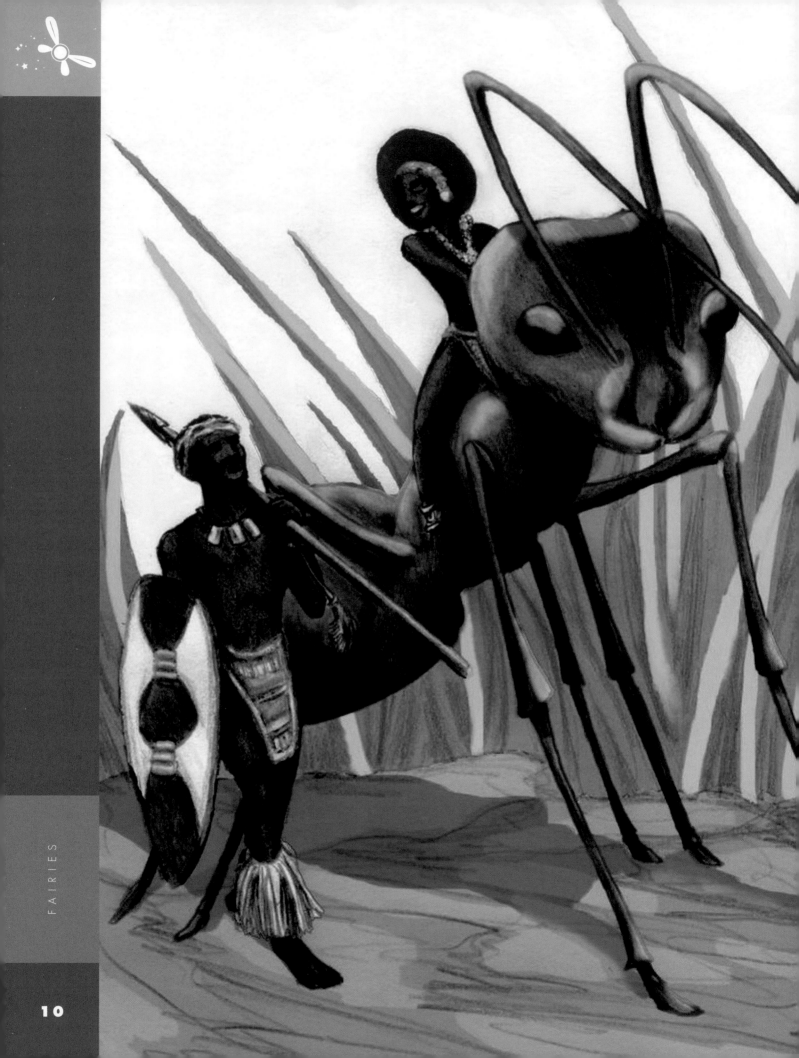

Elves, pixies, and leprechauns belong to the fairy family. Banshees are scary Irish fairies. They scream to let people know something bad will happen. Aziza are West African fairies. They live in anthills. Their magic helps hunters.

Stories from West Africa told of Aziza who taught people about fire and helpful plants.

In England, hawthorn is said to be haunted by fairies.

Fairies

Fairies build their homes under mounds of earth. **Hawthorn** marks the way into the fairy world. These places are called fairy forts. Some people thought fairy forts were special places. In Ireland, people do not move what is left of the fairy forts.

hawthorn a thorny bush whose leaves and berries are used in some medicines

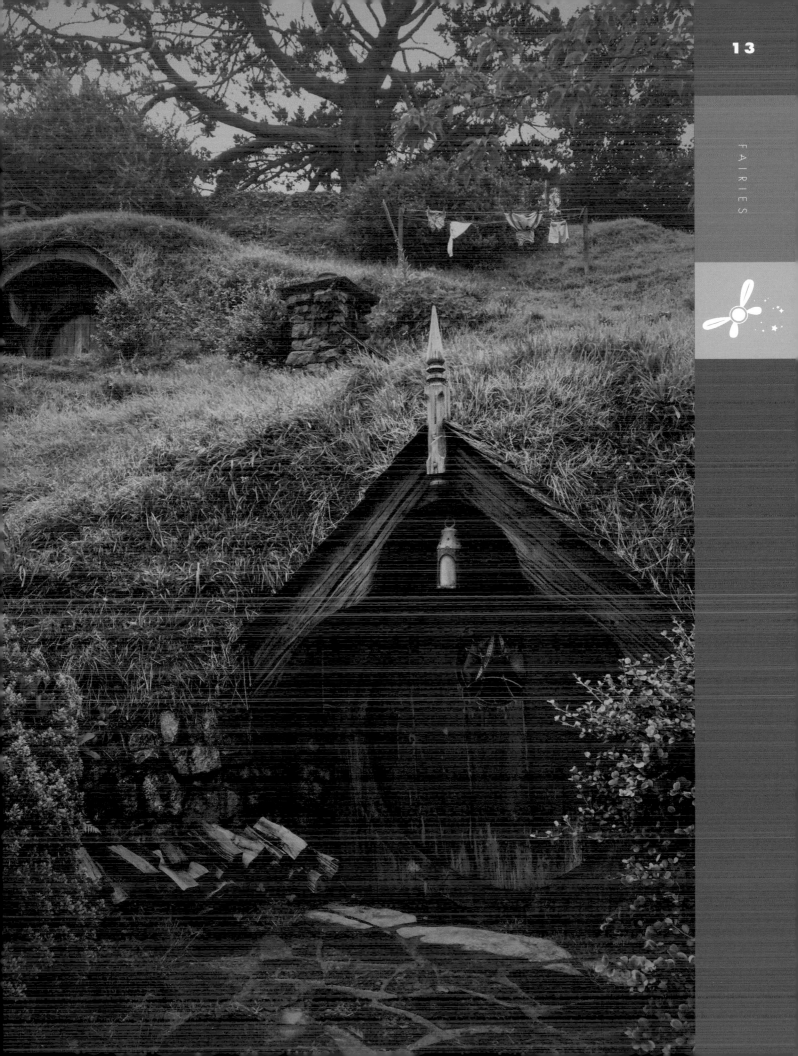

Fairies honor the start of summer with a parade. It is called the fairy rade. They wear fine clothing. They dress up the animals they ride. Even witches and goblins join the fun.

After their parade, the fairies have a feast.

Under a full moon, fairies dance inside fairy rings. These are formed by mushrooms or moss growing in a circle. Stories say that stepping into fairy rings brings bad luck.

Some mushrooms grow in rings or arcs in forests and in grasslands.

Cousins Elsie Wright and Frances Griffiths (pictured) claimed the fairies were real for a long time.

In 1917, two girls in England reported seeing fairies. They took photographs of them. The famous Cottingley Fairies turned out to be a **hoax**. They were made of cardboard.

hoax a joke or prank

Storybook fairies include

Tinker Bell and the fairy godmothers
of Cinderella and Sleeping Beauty. On
television, Abby Cadabby the fairy lives on
Sesame Street.

*Unlike other fairies,
fairy godmothers were
helpful creatures.*

A Fairy Story

A fairy led his three youngsters into a meadow. He plucked a dandelion that had gone to seed. The young fairies watched as he blew on the fluffy white dandelion. The seeds exploded in a flurry. Each young fairy grabbed one. The breeze lifted them off the ground. The fairies flapped their lacy wings. The dandelion seeds helped them stay aloft. Their laughter echoed across the meadow. This is how fairies learn to fly.

Read More

Hawkins, Emily. *A Natural History of Fairies*. London: Quarto, 2020.

London, Martha. *Fairies*. Minneapolis: Pop!, 2020.

Murray, Laura K. *Fairies*. Mankato, Minn.: Creative Education, 2017.

Websites

Fact Monster: Fairies
https://www.factmonster.com/features/creature-catalog/fairies
Learn about fairies and their relatives.

Kiddle: Fairy Facts for Kids
https://kids.kiddle.co/Fairy
Read about fairies in history.

Index